How I Reduce, Reuse, and Recycle

by Robin Nelson

first step nonfiction

Lerner Publications Company · Minneapolis

LERNER

SOURCE

Expand learning beyond the printed book. Download free, complementary educational resources for this book from our website, www.lernersource.com.

The images in this book are used with the permission of: © Todd Strand/Independent Picture Service.

Front Cover: © Laura Westlund/Independent Picture Service.

Main body text set in ITC Avant Garde Gothic Std Medium 21/25.
Typeface provided by Adobe Systems.

Lerner Publications Company
A division of Lerner Publishing Group, Inc.
241 First Avenue North
Minneapolis, MN 55401 USA

For reading levels and more information, look up this title at www.lernerbooks.com.

Library of Congress Cataloging-in-Publication Data

Nelson, Robin, 1971– author.
    How I reduce, reuse, and recycle / by Robin Nelson.
        pages   cm. — (First step nonfiction. Responsibility in action)
    Includes index.
    ISBN 978–1–4677–3636–7 (lib. bdg. : alk. paper)
    ISBN 978–1–4677–3643–5 (eBook)
    1. Waste minimization—Juvenile literature. 2. Recycling (Waste, etc.)—Juvenile literature.
3. Salvage (Waste, etc.)—Juvenile literature. I. Title.
TD793.9.N445 2014
363.72'8—dc23   2013030154

Manufactured in the United States of America
1 – BP – 12/31/13

Table of Contents

Caring for Earth

I want to care for the
planet.

I will start at home.

First, I **reduce** the trash I make.

6

I drink from a glass instead
of a plastic water bottle.

Getting Started

Solitaire

Magnifier

Microsoft Office 2010

Apple Software Update

▸ All Programs

🔍

Control Panel

Devices and Printers

Default Programs

Help and Support

Shut down ▸

I reduce the **energy** and water I use.

I turn off lights I'm not using.

I turn off drippy faucets.

Let's Reuse

Next, I **reuse**.

I give my brother an old
T-shirt that doesn't fit me.

I make a bird feeder out
of a milk jug.

Let's Recycle

Finally, I **recycle**.

I collect cans, bottles, and paper.

ıt them in the recycling

A truck takes them to a **plant** where they become something new.

17

That's how I care for the planet at home.

How would you do it?

Activity

Write a Story

Pretend that you are responsible for reducing, reusing, and recycling in your home. On a separate sheet of paper, write a story about the steps that you would take to do this job. Use at least three of the words shown on the opposite page to write your story.

Story Word List

first

next

then

last

before

after

finally

Fun Facts

- Most US homes recycle 900 aluminum cans a year!

- You can recycle cans, bottles, glass, paper, magazines, paper and plastic bags, batteries, video games, and even your old TV! Find out which items can be recycled where you live.

- Recycling one aluminum can saves enough energy so that you can listen to 10 songs on an MP3 player.

Glossary

energy – usable power

plant – a building where something is made

recycle – to use trash such as glass, plastic, and cans to make new products

reduce – to make smaller in size, amount, or number

reuse – to find a new way to use something instead of throwing it away

Index